Contents

There are those who make things happen

There are those who watch things happen

There are those who wonder what happened

Introduction

By now your child or children have probably already taken some exams and tests while at school, and had various results, some good and maybe some bad. Perhaps you didn't need to worry too much about the results. But as they come up to their major exams the subject becomes a bit more serious because these results can affect their lives and future, and it will be a new and possibly rather more frightening time for them.

Are you going to hope that it all just happens OK, and leave them to struggle alone? Do you propose to leave it to the teachers and then put the blame on the school if your child does badly?

Or, as a parent, do you think you should try to help?

Up until now their school life has been fairly carefree – have the right books on the day, get the homework done, don't be late for class and so on. They haven't had to think very far ahead for themselves – you and the teachers have done most of that for them. But now things are changing. The children as individuals must now carry a bit more responsibility. They are going to have to take it seriously, discipline themselves, plan their time and use it effectively, and gear themselves up to undertake a major task. In many ways preparing themselves to take exams is a part of growing up. It doesn't mean that they can't have any fun anymore, but it does mean that they have to start taking a part of their life *more* seriously.

There is a lot written these days on the subject of education, and all kinds of politics and wrangling seems to go on year after year. But one aspect always remains:

Children who get the help and support of their parents consistently do better at school than those children for whom home support doesn't happen.

What can I do?

You can help your child to take on the burden of preparing for the exams. Once in that exam hall they are on their own. So they need to get themselves ready, and this book is to help you to help them do that. Its purpose is to give you, the parent, a toolkit that you and your child can use together so that you give him/her the best support that you can. Although you may not be that good at a particular subject yourself, you can still help enormously with the revision and learning by organising the time and workspace so that your child can get on with the task. In addition there are a whole lot of techniques that you can pass on that will be invaluable for them.

So while the teachers are concentrating on the academic syllabus, the role you can play as parent(s) is as a coach and a facilitator – you can help get the obstacles out of the way, you can make it easy for the necessary self-discipline to develop, you can keep spirits and morale up, and boost your child's confidence and motivation.

Even just showing an interest makes a difference, but if in addition you can give your child an ordered and calm way to set about this phase of their life, a checklist or two so that they know they haven't missed out vital elements, and a receptive ear to their needs, you will have done a lot. Don't underestimate the importance of morale. Any child undertaking something for the first time likes a helping hand, and any pupil will feel and do far better if the family is supporting his/her efforts.

Sometimes you will hear the excuse '… just isn't any good at exams.' Don't accept this. Exam-taking can be mastered. Candidates can get prepared and build up their confidence, practice papers can be sat, techniques can be learnt.

You can help by showing that you understand the difference between being good at a subject and being 'good at exams', and that both are important.

Some of the reasons to support the idea of getting good at exams are given next, as you consider some of life's 'Realities'.

Some Realities (1)

1. There will always be exams.

Although 'continuous assessment', involving the evaluation of coursework, has over recent years become much more common as part of examinations, many courses and skill levels are still assessed by exam papers and will continue to be so. Fashions change, exam styles change, and the curriculum to be studied can alter, but sooner or later students have to show that their studied material has been memorised, learnt and understood, and can be recalled. This has been a part of study and education for centuries. Other skills may come to be added to those of numeracy and literacy, for example IT and communication skills, but these will often be subject to testing in broadly similar ways.

2. Exams need to be passed!

People and organisations in the world around you want to know if your child has skills and abilities that are useful to them. One way they can find out is to see what exams your child has taken and passed. If he/she hasn't taken or passed any exams, then they will tend to think he/she doesn't have any skills, and the people next in the queue, the ones with the exam certificates, will get first chance at the interesting jobs. Your child may be a King of the PlayStation, brilliant on a skateboard or a netball hotshot, but he/she needs to take and pass exams in order to pave a way in life.

3. They need to learn how!

There's no great mystery to exams, and there's no need to be afraid of them. But there's more to passing them than just being 'good at' the subject. There's a way of approaching the whole process that the pupils need to know as well. They need to know what they should know, certainly, but you can also make sure your child builds up their confidence so that they are ready for the exams without being stressed, and they don't panic on the day.

It's important that they manage themselves through the exam process, as well as mastering the subjects as best they can. This is a life skill that they need to pick up, and as a parent it's your job to help them with that.

4. Skills take time!

This isn't really the book to be opened for the first time the day before the exam. If you are going to climb a big mountain you prepare for months, getting yourself fit, getting your equipment together, studying the terrain, and so on. Exams are the same, the student needs to get ready in plenty of time, and this book takes the two-year period up to GCSEs as its time frame. One of the best ways to get ready is to practise.

5. Practise.

It's hard to sharpen a skill unless you put the practice hours in, and taking exams is no different. Your child needs to be thinking about it and getting familiar with the process so that he/she will be relaxed and able to focus on the questions, and not be put off by imaginary pressure, or the strangeness of the exam hall, or other people's nerves. Practise (such as mock exams) is good. Treat 'mocks' like a training session.

6. Exams aren't just a school thing!

Education goes on long after school days are over and your children are going to find all sorts of exams cropping up in their lives. You have to take a theory test to get a driving licence, for example. Universities and colleges have exams, training courses have exams, and many professions have entrance exams. Being examined and taking tests is part of life, so the life skill of exam-sitting will continue to be useful.

A very necessary development that will need to occur is that of getting organised. You will be wise to lay your hands on some ring binders, a hole punch, some section separators and so on. Filing is not something young people are particularly used to (or inclined towards) but you are going to need some basic office supplies – the school will probably have some recommendations here.

Essential Information (2)

For any subject on which there's to be an exam, it is important to know exactly what the student is going to be required to do, and when. You need to make sure you have found this out at the beginning of the course rather than discovering it much later on, or as the course goes along. Part of the key to success is making a study plan, so you need this information earlier rather than later.

Firstly you will need a copy of the syllabus for each of the subjects that are to be taken. Without this you won't know which aspects of the subject are going to be examined. So if six subjects are to be taken you'll need a syllabus for each. The teachers should provide these but remind your child to ask for them.

Secondly, you will need to find out what form the examination takes. You need to know if any coursework has to be submitted or any modular tests or internal exams taken. You'll need to know what form these assessments will take, when they will occur, about the final exam papers and any oral or practical assessments at the end of the course. The teachers should have this information.

Once you have this you will be able to help your child to produce an overall calendar for studies. Obtain a large sheet of paper or card (A1) and rule it up so that the major tasks and events can be plotted up and seen on a week by week or month by month basis. It will more than likely have to be amended as time goes on, it's astonishing how seeing the whole picture makes the task start to appear manageable.

Incidentally, make sure that you're not the one who makes up the chart. If your child does this then there is a psychological acceptance process that takes place … 'getting your head round it' really is an important part of building exam confidence.

In addition, it will also be essential to find out what the main textbooks are so that you can acquire them or secure access to them. If there is a list of further references it would be good to get hold of this also.

Finally, you need to enquire about past examination papers, specimen papers and marking schemes (see separate section). Try to find out also if any examiners' reports on previous examinations are available. These will help you to find out what the examiners are looking for. It's as critical for the student to know how to answer the question as it is to know the answer.

Teachers and/or tutors should provide you with this essential information – it's part of their responsibility. However, there is nothing to stop you writing to the examining authority directly – you can get the address from your child's school or college, or look it up in your local library, also a lot of very good material can be found on the Internet.

Self-Motivation and Discipline (3)

There is hard work to be done and for success to be had it will be necessary to keep up the motivation. Part of it may come from interest in the subjects, but this is obviously going to vary between subjects. But a strong motive to succeed is going to be needed if your child is going to keep up the necessary drive over say, two years, and so some goal-setting will be needed. This is not necessarily familiar territory for your child, and as parent you may need to help.

A goal can be a long-term goal (I want to be an astronaut), an esteem goal (I want to be top of the class), a belonging goal (I want to be like my big sisters who all got straight 'A's), but the safety goal (I have to do well or my parents will be cross) probably will not work as it lacks positivity. The long-term goals don't always last either, and can weaken or change, and you may find yourself needing to reinforce them from time to time by confirming that his/her goal is your goal too (I also want you to be an astronaut / be top / equal big sisters' records).

It may not be easy to help pick out a long-term goal. Most boys would rather see themselves as a star footballer than an office worker, but reality is that there are going to be more office workers than football stars.

To be a star footballer you probably have to begin showing proficiency at the age of about six, so the chance may already have been missed.

One classic long-term goal for many pupils has been to go to university, but this is by no means a universal desire.

Sadly, the 'X-Factor' type of talent contests on TV, promising instant success and celebrity, do not help your child to set goals. The 'Money for Jam' ethos generates plenty of false goals, and promises reward for no work, which is not helpful when trying to focus on the exam curriculum.

But if you can't help your child settle on a long-term goal, try an esteem or belonging goal (You show 'em! or Make the family proud!).

You may also have to help your child by encouraging and recommending some short-term goals, (milestones) for the week, for the study session, etc. Milestones can be a big help as they get your child feeling confident through a sense of achievement. But they also signal the point at which you can put relaxations and distractions into the plan. Though the primary need is to study, a set discipline that says, for example, 'complete the two revision topics, then have a half-hour football kickabout', or 'complete the write-up of the essay notes and then have a music session', will keep study and relaxation in perspective.

Effective Studying (4)

Exams require your child to remember and recall things, and for this your child has to study. There just isn't any way round this, and no instant solution. What you can do however is try to make sure that the study time is used in the most efficient and effective way, and that it becomes an accepted routine rather than a hated chore.

So how can this best be done?

Firstly it's essential to establish an organised study routine. This means setting aside regular times for study, and nothing short of an emergency should be allowed to intrude on them. You can help a lot here by making sure the household schedule and timings fit in with your child's study schedule and helping to maintain the routine, such as: home from school---cup of tea---period of study---supper---period of study---relaxation---bed. It won't always work, and there will be disruptions, but these occasions should be the exceptions.

Your child also needs an appropriate place. The ideal physical environment is as follows:

■ It is comfortable and suitably warm.

■ It is well-ventilated and well-lit.

■ It is quiet and free of distraction.

■ It has adequate working space.

There are plenty of other attributes one can think of, naturally, but even the elements above are not necessarily easy to provide in the average family house. If your child has his/her own bedroom then you may choose to make some changes to the study area … a raised bunk bed that provides a workspace beneath it is quite an effective solution to the requirement, but other distractions in the room will have to be managed. If there is space to keep reference books, files, previous work and notes, then so much the better.

One of the important benefits of having an appropriate study space is that it makes it easier for your child to get into a routine, and for the rest of the household to get used to the routine as well. There may well be some initial friction as the new arrangement affects others in the family, so you'll need to help your child through this.

A key element for effective study is for your child to have a positive attitude. Try to reinforce the positive attitude with your own, and remember there will probably be times when it will need some extra propping up.

Habits of regular study do tend to bring their own rewards in the form of satisfaction and sense of achievement, like the completion of an assignment on time or a good grade in an assessment. However, you can also add some rewards into the process such as small treats when targets have been met or expectations exceeded. A bar of chocolate when your child gets a better-than-expected result on a homework assignment does no harm at all, and reinforces the message that you are there supporting his/her efforts.

The most important way you can help your child is to help him/her to develop and adopt effective study habits. This is not an easy thing to do. There may be habits to break and behaviour that needs to change, and the list of necessary qualities may seem hopelessly long, but you being aware of these qualities is a start.

Read the list below and see how many elements you can actually help with – as for the rest, well, your child's going to have to manage those alone, with as much encouragement as you can provide.

Qualities of an effective student

- Is organised.
- Produces study timetables with specific goals.
- Studies at regular times.
- Studies in a suitable place.
- Has a positive attitude.

18

- Rewards himself/herself for success.

- Settles quickly to work.

- Devotes sufficient time to study.

- Gives adequate time to difficult/uninteresting topics.

- Notes the advice given by tutors.

- Considers the ideas of fellow students.

- Asks for help when it is needed.

- Produces careful notes.

- Revises work regularly.

- Maintains an interest in his/her studies.

- Sets aside time to relax.

- Eats and drinks sensibly.

- Builds on his/her strong points.

- Keeps things in perspective.

- Refuses to be disturbed during study sessions.

- Obtains all the information that he/she needs.

- Maintains a level of motivation.

- Sets clear deadlines.

- Turns off the music when studying.

- Turns off the TV when studying.

- Turns off the mobile phone while studying.

- Plans the study schedule so that things aren't left to the last minute.

- Has a determination to succeed.

20

Keeping Healthy (5)

Keeping healthy is something to aim for all the time of course, but your child needs to be on top form for effective studying, and may not be able to fulfil potential if tired, run down, or suffering from a succession of minor ailments like colds and flu. This is particularly important during the period leading up to the exams. Being on good form mentally is equally important and your child needs to be as free as possible from worry and anxiety, to have a positive sense of self worth and confidence, to be able to handle the pressure and anticipation sensibly and rationally, whilst still being able to enjoy life and friendships.

Obviously individual circumstances vary and not every child is fortunate enough to enjoy physical health to the full. Nor is it possible to always be able to avoid the emotional stresses that are so often a fact of life amongst the young. But it's worth being aware that the exam phase of life places an additional burden on your child's emotional life and that it's necessary to take whatever steps possible to ensure a high degree of fitness for the course in general and the exam period in particular.

Some extra emphasis on 'wellness for the exams', with a good-natured focus on diet, exercise and good sleep patterns will help to introduce a sensible regime which your child can perhaps be encouraged to follow.

This is not the place to define a well-balanced natural diet, but sufficient to say that it is important for your child to eat healthily. There is a temptation to consume too much coffee and tea during lengthy revision periods, and these excite rather than calm the nerves. A carton of fruit juice is a better thing to have in the house.

Recognise that it is a stressful time for your child and there are a host of unknown fears to be faced. Try to help him/her find a means of positive relaxation, whether it's yoga, music, jogging, jiving, etc. Ration it sensibly, but recognise that it is necessary.

Try to make sure your child gets regular and sufficient sleep. An occasional late night should not be a problem, but if it happens frequently it may certainly become one. If sleep is a problem, try to encourage finding a solution in a relaxation method rather than resorting to pills.

Do encourage your child to exercise regularly. It improves powers of concentration and sense of well-being. Half an hour's football or a brisk jog around the block each day will do wonders for the circulation and help the brain function.

Try to protect your child from damaging emotional problems, as far as you can. It is not the time to present your child with problems that can wait until after the exams are over. There are a host of added tensions present as a result of the studies, so try to reduce the effect of things likely to add to them. A certain mild level of anxiety is perfectly normal, even helpful, at examination time, but for the maximum chance of success your child needs to remain as positive, calm and healthy as possible.

There are a number of books and publications about diet, relaxation, etc, and it may help to consult some of them. If you feel that professional advice is needed, your child should consult a doctor or the college health practitioner.

Taking and Keeping Notes (6)

Has anyone discussed note-taking with your child? Note-taking is a skill that can be practised, and your child may well need some pointers as to how best to do it.

It's a good skill to develop because:

- It helps the listener to pay attention.

- It helps to organise one's thoughts and ideas.

- It records the information presented.

- It helps the reader remember the information.

- It builds a revision tool.

Not everyone finds note-taking easy, whether it is from a spoken lecture or from a book. There are all kinds of note-taking techniques and many university publications on the subject can be found on the Internet. One of the most powerful note-taking tools is the Mind-Map, which encourages the listener to record relevant ideas in a graphical diagram that is easily recalled, and this is taught in many schools. It needs some practise to become skilled, along with some trial and error, and not everyone likes it, but it is a very powerful technique that your child should at least try out.

Whatever note-taking technique is to be used, the aim is the same. The most important items must be identified and recorded in such a way that the presented material can be reconstructed from the notes taken. They only need to be read by the note taker who can use a completely personalised system provided it works. However, notes need to have certain key attributes:

- Easily read.

- Brief.

- Clear.

- Useful.

- Organised.

■ Relevant.

Most schools and tutors give some guidance on note-taking and the best help you can give your child is to try to discuss the guidance and see if the suggested methods are going to be helpful, or at least given a try. If note-taking as a topic seems too vague and abstract, then it might help your child if you pick out a subject where notes have been taken and see whether they have been understood, and if they have the key attributes as above. See how well your child can make sense of the notes because this can help to find flaws in the note-taking which can then be fixed.

Usually tutors are happy to review their students' note-taking and to give advice, so if you think your child is finding note-taking hard it should be easy to get some extra help. This will pay big dividends later and is worth doing.

Some subjects will require more elaborate notes than others. However, all notes will need some tidying work if the material is to be something which helps at revision time. The best habit to have is one where your child reviews the notes the same day they were taken, amends them as appropriate and then files them. This will provide four very important effects:

■ Reviewing the subject the same day reinforces the learning.

■ Tidying the notes increases the understanding.

■ Gaps in understanding can be identified and noted as questions for the teacher.

■ A better revision tool is created for later use.

Reviewing and writing up notes is best if treated as an automatic homework assignment. 'Self-imposed homework' is not the easiest habit for your child to form so you will probably have to give some encouragement for this along the lines of 'Do it before you forget it'.

With writing-up, remind your child that the notes are going to be used later for revision, so it's just as well to get the ideas down clearly.

'Write them so that someone else can understand them, then you will be able to understand them yourself later on.'

Note taking from textbooks or reference books is slightly different in that the student is not recording material 'in-flight'. Making notes in one's own words at the end of a section or chapter is well known to be one of the most effective ways to study. The action of re-phrasing the content actually causes a thinking and remembering process (copying the textbook out word for word is not nearly as effective) and also helps in the creative process that will become essays at exam time.

Another good thing for your child to remember is to put references in his/her notes. If during revision there turns out to be something on which more depth is needed, and it's necessary to go back to the original book, then a link to the chapter and page can save hours of scratching about – it's also handy if references have to be quoted in essays.

Textbook notes also need to be assembled in some kind of a framework (the subject teacher can help here) so that they can be filed and retrieved later on as revision items. Use chapter headings and sub-headings from the textbook, or website references, if they fit in with the overall syllabus. A diagram is a good idea as it can be added to as the study year goes on.

It's good to space out notes on the page because it makes them easier to scan and to amend if necessary. It's best to file them in a loose-leaf ring binder as this makes it easier to add later items in the right place. Other pages, such as handouts from tutors, can also be filed there, and hard copies of material downloaded from the Internet can be inserted also.

Every student has his or her own way of setting up files and notes, and the school or college may also have some advice, but be prepared to spend a few pounds on office equipment such as ring binders, a hole punch, separators, etc, and encourage your child to get a system going early. One binder per subject is a start, but there may be a need for more than one binder for some subjects.

Some students will prefer to keep all their notes on their computer so that they can share them with colleagues by emailing useful items to each other. There's nothing wrong with this just as long as their system has the key attributes – in fact MS Windows can do a lot of the organising very effectively.

Essay Writing (7)

The ability to write essays is an important skill to have. Examiners like to test using essay questions because they not only test the candidate's knowledge but also the candidate's ability to think through the knowledge and present it clearly.

Some students find essay writing difficult and demanding. However, there is a way of going about it that makes it much easier. Whether your child finds essays easy or hard, it's a good idea to go through this section together. You may find that your child already does all or part of what is suggested here, but still there may well be some extra hints to follow.

There is a successful 'how to' formula that can be applied to essay writing, which helps to make the job much easier:

■ Read and understand the question.

■ Plan out your response from start to finish.

■ Check that it answers the question.

■ Check that the sequence makes good sense.

And then

■ Write out the essay.

■ Read it through.

The essay itself needs an introduction, a main body and a conclusion. The components have contents as follows:

a. Introduction

Puts the question in context, explains briefly what the main points are and outlines the conclusion. This is the point at which the writer can make an extra check that the question as set is being answered.

b. Main body

This is a series of paragraphs, in a logical sequence, that cover each of the main ideas that are to be presented in answer to the question. Each main idea should have a paragraph of its own and relate to the main points that were outlined in the introduction.

c. Conclusion

This refers to the question as it was set and explains how the points made in the main body have answered it. Note that if an opinion is invited in the question (e.g. to agree or disagree) then the opinion should reflect the arguments that have been made in the main body. It is perfectly acceptable to neither agree nor disagree if the arguments seem to be balanced – the exercise is in formulating and presenting the arguments, not whether the examiner agrees with the candidate's opinion.

Reading it through

This is the opportunity to correct any spelling or grammatical errors and cross out any rough workings. The essential thing at this point is to make the work as easy as possible for the examiner to read.

Most essay questions, whether they are part of coursework or part of a final exam paper, can be approached using the formula above. Essay writing is a skill, which means it can be improved with practise. It's a useful skill in many areas of later life so encourage your child to practise, under simulated exam conditions if possible, so that the technique becomes familiar and the approach is automatic.

Coursework Assignments (8)

Many subjects include special projects or assignments, which are assessed and marked separately from the exam process.

If this is the case then it is important to know exactly what the coursework assignments are, what form they are to take, how long will be allowed for them to be completed, when they have to be handed in and what percentage marks they contribute towards the final grade. Once you know this the tasks need to be scheduled into the timetable.

By far and away the biggest problem that occurs with coursework tasks is that students do not allocate enough time to complete them. They tend to underestimate the time they need for an assignment, and often because it is a big undertaking they tend to put off starting it. It is also true that to have to manage a project like this can be an unknown experience, so you can help if you provide some kind of a model or framework. At least if you can suggest that your child breaks the project up into stages and sets completion targets to each stage then you will have pointed him/her in the right direction.

A key reason for this is to make sure that handing-in (submission) deadlines are met without panic, last-minute rush and the inevitable compromise of quality and marks.

Coursework assignments are a very good way to earn high marks but they need to be compiled in an organised fashion.

Here is a general schedule which will help focus ideas as to how to set about the project:

- a) Agree the scope.

- b) Carry out the study.

- c) Assemble the information.

- d) Complete the first draft.

- e) Produce the completed assignment.

Note that each of these stages can be reviewed with the tutor, who can then provide guidance and direction on how to improve the final submission. By getting feedback on stages (a) to (d) well in advance of any deadline your child will be able to correct errors or gaps and so turn in a respectable submission. Other things can go wrong of course, but finding a glaring omission halfway through writing up the final draft is not bad luck, it's bad organisation.

The best contribution you can make is to talk through the elements (a) to (e) above and help your child to set them into a schedule. A week might be suitable for phase (a), two weeks possibly needed for each of (b) and (c), a week for (d), leaving two weeks for the final version (e) and any polishing.

Often tutors will have several pupils with coursework projects, all of whom will be expecting various reviews and feedback. All tutors have time constraints, so getting your feedback sessions in early, before the rush, will get your child a better use of the tutor's time.

Encourage your child to make a start on the assignment as soon as it has been given out. Time will be needed to think it over, make notes about any aspects that need to be queried and generally set about the first phase of agreeing the scope. This may well require discussions with colleagues or the teacher/tutor, and if so remind your child to make good notes about what is agreed. Notes on the scope will probably be needed as an appendix for the final submission in any event, but they will also come in handy before then as a checklist.

Having a well-described scope and specification will make the next phase a lot simpler. The research, information gathering, experimentation or whatever the assignment entails will be defined as a relevant item within the scope of the content, and will be that much easier to understand and appreciate. The whole study phase will become much easier to undertake and to complete because your child has a clear overall idea of what has to be done. This will also mean that the right emphasis will be placed on important content, and your child won't be tempted to waste time or become sidetracked.

Your child may need some help getting hold of the material needed. The tutors should be able to help here, but if you have some Internet skills you may be able to lend a hand yourself. Make sure your child knows that you are ready to add some support if it is needed.

As the time comes to write the first draft it may be useful to remind your child of good essay writing techniques – nothing helps the writing task more than a good outline plan, and this can take the form of notes, mind-maps or whatever method your child finds most helpful. However, it's also important to make it as tidy as possible – the idea is to get helpful feedback from the tutor, and if the draft work is hard to decipher it will make an evaluation task harder for the teacher, so the advice may not be as helpful. Criticisms about legibility or presentation are not nearly as useful as suggestions as to possible content to be added, or other ways to approach an analysis.

Make sure also that you are invited to read both the first draft and the final submission – your show of interest will boost the morale of your child. It will also help your child to see that coursework is not just a burden, but something that you think is important – as indeed it is.

It's not possible to leave the subject of coursework without discussing the use of the Internet. Masses of information on a coursework topic can be accessed in a few moments, and there is nothing wrong in that. Looking things up in encyclopaedias is not that different. The trap to avoid is thinking that simply cutting and pasting the material from websites will meet the coursework requirements. The likelihood is that the question is framed in such a way that original work will be required, so the test is not how well your child handles Google but how the material located is assessed, assembled, evaluated and presented.

There may be temptations to try to short cut the work and plagiarise, but as a rule these submissions are very easy to spot, and will attract low marks. If your child wants to get good grades, and wants to use the coursework results to help get them, then it is undoubtedly better to hand in original work, but (of course) acknowledging referenced sources.

Past Exam Papers (9)

The exam authorities are constantly revising and updating both their syllabus contents and their assessment methods, and your child may even be among the first to sit an exam in its new form. Access to old papers also depends on the policy of the examining authority and whether they are in print or not.

Nevertheless, you should make every effort to ensure that your child has access to as many past or sample examination papers as possible. The tutors/teachers should have at least some of those that are available, but if not you can write to the examining authority directly. Your child should have the papers that are exactly in the form that is to be met in the actual exam, so if the form has changed recently make sure the sample papers are in the new form. Papers used before that time may be helpful but should be used with caution as, for example, they may cover topics that are no longer in the syllabus. If the exam is in a new form then the examining authority will almost certainly have produced a sample paper.

In addition to gaining access to past papers the teachers/tutors should be able to acquire the appropriate marking schemes. This again will depend on the policy of the examining authority but if available they will provide a great deal of insight into the kind of answers examiners are looking for. Some good guidance should come from the teachers/tutors in any event, and, if possible, you should study it to a level that you can discuss it with your child, which will be helpful.

It may be necessary to purchase past papers and marking scheme material, in which case be assured that this will be money well spent. A few minutes on the Internet and a quick search of eBay can turn up a wide range of possibilities for you.

The big benefit your child will gain from past papers is that of familiarity. By reading the instructions in several papers, getting a feel for how many questions are to be answered and seeing how much time is allotted, there will be fewer surprises on starting the paper on the day and a calmer and more confident attempt can be made.

Another big help is to get a feel for the style of questions that are to be answered. It will become clear that questions fall into separate sections and follow certain patterns. Your child can become familiar with the particular wordings that are used and understand what is required when questions are worded in slightly different ways.

Past papers also allow candidates to practise. Taking one question at a time, with breaks in-between if necessary, your child can spend half a day doing a complete paper to exam timings, and then hand it in for the tutor's comments. Careful feedback at this point is very helpful both for building confidence and sharpening answering skills.

Past papers will also allow your child to predict likely topics. Nothing can be guaranteed, but if there is a choice of questions and the format has been the same for a number of years, it may be possible to forecast with some accuracy the most likely topics that will come up. This may help focus revision on particular areas because of the high likelihood of there being questions on the given topics, but of course neglecting other areas where there might be a question should be avoided.

The Final Weeks Before the Exam(s) (10)

Helping your child get into the habit of working hard in a disciplined way has been a major theme in this guide. More than anything the final six or eight weeks have a special importance in all those topics and subjects that are to be examined. What is done at this stage can make the difference between a pass and a fail, or between one grade and another.

If you have managed to get your child to follow the advice on previous pages, a good deal of revision has already been done before the final weeks – in fact steady revision has been under way since the original learning of the topic. But even if this has not happened to the extent it perhaps should have, it is possible to raise your child's exam performance considerably by what is done in these few weeks. But the key is not to use the final weeks focussing on new learning or skills, but to concentrate on subject matter previously understood and learnt.

Most schools complete teaching the exam syllabus some weeks before the exams for the express purpose of setting aside a revision phase. The length of the revision period will vary subject by subject, so try to find out where your child is on each – for example, there may be six weeks available to revise Subject A, but the syllabus for Subject B might leave only two weeks for revision, in which case it might be best to try to get Subject A revised and 'bedded down' in time for an effort on Subject B.

As you enter the revision phase it becomes more important than ever to be disciplined and well organised – the teachers can structure things a bit, but your child (with your help) has really got to take over the task in order to meet his/her individual needs. The teacher may be emphasising Topic (i), for example, but your child might be on top of this element but feeling less confident on Topic (ii). The real requirements of the revision phase are therefore highly individual, and only your child really knows where the emphasis needs to be.

If you can lay hands on a summary of the syllabus (and the teachers should be able to help here), you can help your child enormously by having a 'walkthrough' of the syllabus and assigning confidence levels A/B/C/D to various topics. Out of this you can assemble the outline of a very effective revision plan with the key topics scheduled, and even plan to include some tests to help confidence-building.

Another key aspect to address is the time of day that best suits your child for revision. You can help here by adjusting the household timetable around a little to best fit with the revision and homework cycle – and your child will appreciate that an effort is being made to accommodate his/her needs, which will add to the feeling of being supported.

A very good thing to do at this stage is for your child to produce a chart which covers each of the days in these final weeks. The days and times of each of the exam papers can be shown and an overall revision schedule, topic by topic can be written in. The psychological value of this is tremendous. Instead of haphazardly working on topics while worrying about others, your child knows that there is a plan to cover all the topics, and can set about them more calmly. See the table opposite.

Evening Revision Timetable

	Mon	Tues	Wed	Thur	Fri
6.30 - 6.50	Sub. A - Topic i Main points to postcard and learn	Sub. B	Sub. C	Sub. D	Sub. A - Topic iv Discuss with fellow student
6.50 - 7.40	Sub. B	Sub. C	Sub. D	Sub. A - Topic iii Main points to postcard and learn	Sub. B
8.00 - 8.50	Sub. C	Sub. D	Sub. A - Topic i/ii Write main points from memory and check	Sub. B	Sub. C
8.50 - 9.40	Sub. D	Sub. A - Topic ii Learn main points - Test by verbal recall	Sub. B	Sub. C	Sub. D

Weekend Revision Timetable

	Sat	Sun
9.00 - 9.50	Sub. B	Sub. C
9.50 - 10.40	Sub. C	Sub. D
11.00 - 11.50	Sub. D	Sub. A - Topic iii Attempt question from past paper
11.50 - 12.40	Sub. A - Topic i/ii Produce outline answers to two past essay questions	Sub. B

An outline example of a weekly evening and weekend revision timetable. Ideas for revising Subject A have been included.

Active vs passive revision

Something that often gets overlooked is the need to make revision active rather than passive. Rather than reading through notes, your child will absorb far more by doing something positive. Here are some examples that you can encourage.

Self test at regular intervals. This can involve writing out the main points of topics from memory, or writing answers on questions from past or specimen exam papers. Of course, you can help with oral tests where relevant.

Attempting some problems from a different approach. This does not mean addressing a fresh topic so much as applying knowledge to different situations or examples.

Writing out some outline answers to essay questions. Take these from specimen papers or past exam papers if possible.

Verbal recall of the main points of topic notes. This can be helped greatly with good use of 'mind-maps', if the candidate is familiar with this technique.

Postcard notes. Putting topic notes (or mind-maps) onto postcards can be a powerful aid to recall. The action of writing out the card helps to internalise the information and then provides an instant revision tool for spare moments.

Topic discussion. This can be a big help in clarifying learning, particularly if the other person involved asks questions that cause your child to think carefully. You may need to get the help of some of the teachers for this.

Using past papers. There is plenty of nervousness associated with taking exams, and the more this can be reduced by practising the better. Practise will help with timing, with focus on the topic and also familiarisation with a host of secondary factors associated with the whole process. A candidate who has practised taking a two-hour paper many times and knows what to do will often make a better showing than a cleverer candidate who has never been under exam conditions. It is far better to have misread a question while in practice mode, or to have used time badly, than to make this mistake 'on the day'.

Properly done, revision is a time-consuming business, and however much time is put in, and however well-structured and organised the activity, there is always a feeling that more could (or should) have been done. It may help your child to use time better by focussing entirely on a reduced number of topics. If there is to be a choice of questions then there may be some topics that your child will not choose to attempt. It may be possible to be selective in the revision (e.g. I am not going to attempt Topic X so I will not waste time revising it). However, this strategy has some risks associated with it of course, as it restricts choice on the day.

In the final weeks before the examination make sure that you both know where and when the exam will take place. Don't leave this until the last minute, particularly if a different travel arrangement is involved. A rush on the day will cause unnecessary additional stress that is not needed. Some stress and anxiety is inevitable, and even helpful, but a high level will be disruptive and produce poorer results.

Finally, on the night before the examination you must discourage hours and hours of last-minute cramming. If the revision prior to this point has been thorough, it will only need an hour or two to revise and strengthen impressions. However, it is as well to make sure your child has carefully assembled everything that will be needed for the following day – pens, pencils, erasers, ruler, calculator, etc. Better to discover that a protractor has gone missing while there is time to find it, than when you should have left the house 10 minutes ago.

The Day of the Exam (11)

Hopefully you haven't left reading this section until the day itself. Better that you and your child read and reflect upon it several times during the weeks leading up to the big day.

There isn't any new advice in this section, but it does contain suggestions that generations of exam candidates can testify to.

They are presented as a series of do's and don'ts for the examinee, but also indicate where you as a parent can help directly. These are mostly common sense, but well worth thinking about. You need to do what you can to make these suggestions possible. Go through them together.

Do …

Get up early. Much better to have plenty of time to become organised than to be rushing about. Allowing extra time will give your child a better chance of staying calm.

Eat a good breakfast but don't drink too much. Your child doesn't want to be distracted by hunger during the exam, but neither does he/she want to be desperate for the toilet during it.

Remember that some degree of anxiety is quite normal. Calm your child with the thought that proper preparation has been done, and there is every reason that proper justice to their ability will be done. Try to steer any anxiety into anticipation, such as is felt at a sports match or before a stage performance.

Make sure that the essential items for the exam, such as candidate number, pens, erasers, rulers, and spares, are all prepared the night before. This helps instil a feeling of 'I'm ready' and helps relaxed sleep.

Target to be ready at the examination centre 10 minutes before the start time, including a last-minute visit to the toilet. This is long enough to find out where to sit without rushing, but not long enough to hang about worrying and getting nervous.

Suggest your child avoids the crowd and avoids entering into conversations before the start. Better to focus on positive thoughts and stay calm. This is hard to do, but advice such as 'keep your focus and don't get distracted' may help. Importantly, calm advice from you will do much to combat the last-minute nerves.

Be prepared to stay with your child until the last minute, unless this is likely to cause embarrassment (though for every schoolmate that jeers there will be another who feels a bit envious). This can contribute greatly to morale, particularly if the subject is one in which your child lacks confidence.

Remind your child of the key tasks for the first five minutes:

- Read through the entire paper carefully.

- Check if there are any compulsory questions and tick them to do first.

- Double-tick those questions you can answer well.

- Single-tick those you feel you could attempt.

- Cross X those you don't want to attempt.

Application of this relatively simple discipline will give your child a perspective of the paper and some balance in the answers. By doing the preferred questions first, the chances of scoring a better mark is much improved. Try to get this idea accepted early so that the technique can be practised during 'mock' exams, on trial papers, etc.

'Mock' and trial papers also provide a very important opportunity to learn how to manage timing. If the paper is two and a half hours and there are five questions to be answered, your child should work to finish each of the questions in less than half an hour – some time for reading through and correcting is vital. Some practise at home with the kitchen timer is a good investment of time because it gets your child used to the rhythm of sitting a paper. This is an important element to remember on the day, but well worth understanding in advance.

There is an important tactical element to timing also. Tempting as it may be to spend two hours on just three questions to get 18/20 marks, it won't be as effective as spending less time for 15/20 marks, and picking up an additional 7 marks for relatively weak answers to each of two additional questions – the difference might mean a higher grade, or a pass, rather than a fail.

Also note that if there is a mark allocation for each part of a question then the most concentration needs to go into the parts of the question carrying the most marks.

Encourage your child to expunge all thoughts of the exam once out of the exam room. There is nothing more that can be done, and it may well undermine confidence if a post-mortem is undertaken. The results will come in the fullness of time and if the work has been put in effectively they should reflect your child's ability and hard work.

Arrange a little reward when the paper is over. At least encourage some exercise and relaxation – it may be necessary to get ready for another exam paper the next day, so keep the celebration under control, but some mental relaxation is very necessary.

Exam tips for your child

Remember to re-read each question very carefully before starting to write. Identify any key words like 'discuss', 'outline', 'identify' and 'evaluate', and circle them. Think through and take a minute to plan your response before starting your answer.

Remember to always number the question or part of the question that you are answering. If the exam paper asks you to show the numbers of the questions you have answered on the front of the paper then make sure you leave time to do this.

43

Answer the question as set. Resist the temptation to write all that you know about a topic irrespective of what is being asked. You will probably use up more time than the question is worth.

Don't panic if your memory seems to fail you. If what you are trying to remember simply won't come back to you, start another question and come back to the problem later. Don't spend too long on a difficulty, and don't allow yourself to be unsettled by one.

Write as legibly as you can and present your work in a manner that the examiner will find comprehensible. The exam is not a test of handwriting or presentation but the examiner will be more at ease (and more tolerant of minor errors) if your work is clear and easy to follow. Be sure to cross out any rough working, and avoid writing in the margins – leave these for the examiner to use.

Let the examination supervisor know of anything that is disturbing you, such as a noise outside the exam room or another candidate nervously tapping a pen or pencil.

Check your paper at the end and read through what you have written. Even with the best of preparation it is possible to make silly mistakes and these can only be picked up by reading through. If you do find a mistake where you have badly misinterpreted a question, write a brief note under your answer explaining that you realise your error and explaining how you would have answered now that you realise your mistake. You will be given a few marks for your answer at least, rather than a zero score.

Don't be tempted to cheat or to help others to cheat. At best, if caught, your paper will be cancelled. At worst, the examining authority will bar you from all other examinations. The pressures to pass may be intense, but the penalties attached to cheating are far too great. In any case there should be confidence that the good work done to date will pay off. Also, however anti-social it may feel, it's best to ignore all other students in the exam room.

Final Thoughts (12)

Remember that this is only an introductory guide. If your child needs further help make sure that it gets sought out. The tutors and teachers are there to help, and in addition there are a number of more detailed exam guides and study guides on the market, and some good tutorial sessions to be found on the Internet.

Encourage your child to attend classes or lectures, even if these are optional, as frequently as possible. Focussing on the subject together with others helps to expand understanding. Sometimes one student can ask a question that is a massive help to others, and don't forget that there is some extra enthusiasm to be gained from his/her companions (or fellow sufferers!).

Help to keep up the impetus. Some students will say that they are not worried about revision or exam practice, or that they know everything that they will need. That's not how it works. Encourage your child to stay focussed on doing all the work and trying for a star rating.

Keep the tutors and teachers involved by encouraging your child to try extra sample questions and getting the teachers to mark them and comment. Most are keen to help enthusiastic students, and the feedback will be valuable.

Discourage comparisons of performance with those of other students. Individuals are different and some are more gifted than others in certain areas. Encourage your child to set 'personal best' standards and to aim to reach them. A little rivalry is not a bad thing provided it keeps the motivation positive, but it can generate negativity very easily.

Remember there are no short cuts. Success in examinations can only be assured by hard work. The student will need to accept that the work may often be tedious or difficult, and that there will be times when it would be nicer to be doing something else.

Finally, remember to always be positive and to show confidence in your child's abilities. If the work is put in throughout the course, help is sought when needed and effort put into preparation for the exams, then the child will do justice to his/her abilities.

Good luck! And never lose sight of the thought that …

Failing to prepare is preparing to fail.

Help List

Your child's school should be able to provide you with the biggest source of information and support. However, this section provides additional sources that both you and your child may find of benefit. Visiting any good bookshop will also offer the opportunity to browse the large number of study and revision guides available.

For parents

Department for Children, Schools and Families
The UK Government's website for education

Department for Children, Schools and Families, Sanctuary Buildings,
Great Smith Street, London, SW1P 3BT
Tel: 0870 000 2288
info@dcsf.gsi.gov.uk
www.dfes.gov.uk

www.parentlineplus.org.uk

Website for parents to help cope with exam stress

www.schoolsnet.com

Schools guide for parents
150-152 King Street, Hammersmith, London, W6 0QU
Tel: 0208 600 5313

www.schools.co.uk

The schools directory for parents and teachers
Hamilton House Mailings PLC, Earlstree Court, Earlstree Road, Corby, Northants, NN17 4HH

Skills4study

Information on effective study strategies
www.palgrave.com/skills4study/studyskills

The TES

Current news on education
The Times Educational Supplement, Admiral House, 66-68 East Smithfield, London, E1W 1BX
Tel: 020 7782 3000
www.tes.co.uk

For your child

Exams can prove a stressful time to the examinee, as well as the rest of the family. Tutors are there to support your child, though there are plenty of websites that offer both revision tips and guides as well as information about coping with exam pressure.

Coping with exam stress

www.childline.org.uk
www.isma.org.uk/exams
www.mind.org.uk
www.examstress.org.uk

Revision support

www.bbc.co.uk/schools
www.youthinformation.com
www.s-cool.co.uk
www.revision-notes.co.uk
www.revisioncentre.co.uk
www.what2learn.com

For advice on careers please contact www.connexions-direct.com. By selecting Local Connexions you can locate your nearest office where career advisors and information will be available. If you don't have access to the Internet, your child's school, local council or library should be able to provide details of your nearest careers office.

Need - 2 - Know

Other Large Print Titles Include ...

Allergies A Parent's Guide
ISBN 978-1-86144-160-7 £12.99

Autism A Parent's Guide
ISBN 978-1-86144-165-2 £12.99

Drugs A Parent's Guide
ISBN 978-1-86144-136-2 £12.99

Dyslexia A Parent's Guide
ISBN 978-1-86144-138-6 £12.99

Bullying A Parent's Guide
ISBN 978-1-86144-137-9 £12.99

Epilepsy The Essential Guide
ISBN 978-1-86144-152-2 £12.99

Teenage Pregnancy The Essential Guide
ISBN 978-1-86144-139-3 £12.99

Gap Years The Essential Guide
ISBN 978-1-86144-169-0 £12.99

How to Pass Exams A Parent's Guide
ISBN 978-1-86144-140-9 £12.99

Child Obesity A Parent's Guide
ISBN 978-1-86144-141-6 £12.99

Applying for a Job The Essential Guide
ISBN 978-1-86144-180-5 £12.99

ADHD The Essential Guide
ISBN 978-1-86144-145-4 £12.99

Student Cookbook – Healthy Eating
The Essential Guide
ISBN 978-1-86144-146-1 £12.99

Stress The Essential Guide
ISBN 978-1-86144-147-8 £12.99

Your First Pregnancy The Essential Guide
ISBN 978-1-86144-158-4 £12.99

Special Educational Needs A Parent's Guide
ISBN 978-1-86144-149-2 £12.99

The Pill An Essential Guide
ISBN 978-1-86144-150-8 £12.99

University A Survival Guide
ISBN 978-1-86144-153-9 £12.99

Visit **www.need2knowbooks.co.uk** for the full range. To order our titles call **01733 898103**, email **sales@n2kbooks.com** or visit the website. Selected ebooks available online.

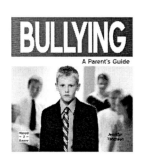
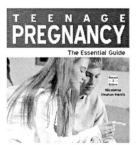

Need - 2 - Know, Remus House, Coltsfoot Drive, Peterborough, PE2 9JX